Short Walks from Wirral Villages

Short Walks from Wirral Villages

Joanna McIlhatton MA

MARA BOOKS

First published in November 2008 by **Mara Books**, 22 Crosland Terrace, Helsby, Frodsham, Cheshire WA6 9LY

All enquiries regarding sales telephone: (01928) 723744

ISBN 978-1-902512-23-5

www.marabooks.co.uk

www.northerneyebooks.com

Contents

Introduction

WITH current concerns over obesity and lack of excercise, there has never been a better time for people to get out into the countryside and walk. Walking is one of the cheapest and simplest forms of recreation and can be shared by almost any age group—it is an ideal family activity. A weekend stroll combined with lunch in a pub or café, or better still a healthy picnic, is the ideal opportunity for everyone to explore Wirral's historic and beautiful countryside.

In Wirral we are fortunate to have on our doorstep one of the best footpath networks in the country which gives easy, free access to a landscape which is both beautiful and varied. Where else can you walk through woods, across farmland, over lowland

Enjoying a walk at Port Sunlight

A family group on the beach at West Kirby

heath with wide open views, along tidal marshes and sandy beaches, and all just a few miles from a major city centre?

Each of the walks in the following pages starts from one of Wirral's many old villages—some are now developed and absorbed into one of the larger towns such as Bromborough or Birkenhead, while others have remained much as they were over a century ago, such as the picturesque village of Burton.

Each walk has something of interest to discover—you will visit the site of an ancient port now completely dried out and over a mile inland; a seafront with neither sand nor sea; a wild, wooded river valley in the heart of industrial Merseyside and a lowland heath with wide views to the Welsh hills—so don some comfortable footwear and get walking.

The walks vary in distance from about 1 to 4¾ miles (1.5km to about 7.5km) and are deliberately undemanding, so even if you are not a regular walker, you will find these walks easy and other than comfortable footware you will need no specialist equipment.

Some walks can only be accessed by car, but many can be reached by public transport. Public transport options are included in the introductions to each chapter. Phone Mersey Travel for information on all bus, train and ferry services on: 0870 608 2608. All the walks in this book are covered by the large scale Ordnance Survey Explorer map sheet 266 Wirral & Chester. The grid references given at the start of each walk refer to this map.

The old seafront at Parkgate

A Map of Wirral and the location of the Walks

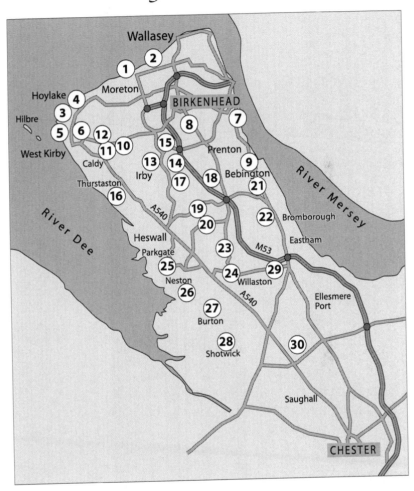

WALK 1

Leasowe & Moreton

This walk visits Leasowe Lighthouse, where it joins the embankment to follow part of the North Wirral Coastal Park Path as far as Leasowe Castle Hotel. A return is made through Moreton.

Start: *Leasowe Lighthouse. Grid ref: 253 913.*

Distance: *5.25km/3¼ miles.*

Parking: *Park in the car park at the end of 'Pasture Road' near the embankment.*

Using public transport: *From Moreton railway station (Mersey Rail), turn right and walk along 'Pasture Road' until you see a footpath/cycle path sign on your left. Take this path and walk across to the lighthouse.*

Refreshments: *Leasowe Castle Hotel.*

Points of Interest: *Leasowe Lighthouse; Nature Trail; Leasowe Castle Hotel*

Leasowe lighthouse is a well known landmark in Wirral. It stands 101 feet high and has seven floors reached by a cast iron staircase of 130 steps. Above the door are the initials, MWG, for the Mayor of Liverpool of the time, William Gregson. The date of 1763, if correct, probably makes it the oldest brick-built lighthouse in Europe. It houses the visitor centre for the North Wirral Coastal Park. An information board to one side tells the history of the lighthouse which is open to the public as follows: April – Sept. 1st & 3rd Sundays 1pm – 4pm; Oct. – March   1st Sunday 1pm – 4pm.

The walk

Turn right out of the car park and walk along the road past the lighthouse. Continue ahead along the track and take the right fork. You are now on the North Wirral Coastal Park path. Pass the pond on your left with ducks, coots etc., part of a local nature trail. Soon the path runs close to the embankment on your right and at sleeper steps, turn right onto the embankment. (If you want to extend the walk you could continue for another 3/4 mile to Dove Point before joining the embankment.) Turn right and walk along the concrete embankment or the grassy area alongside it.

This embankment was built as a defence against the sea and a protection for all the low-lying land in this area. Before the embankment was built, the sea regularly flooded the land at high tide and consequently, the clay soil was improved with the addition of sand and silt to such an extent that the market gardens in the area are famed for early new potatoes and other vegetables.

In the summer of 1962, the world's first hovercraft service began as a trial between the foreshore below Leasowe Common and Rhyl. This little bit of local history is remembered in part of an exhibition in the visitor's centre.

11

Walking near Leasowe Lighthouse

Continue on along the path or embankment to Leasowe Castle Hotel, the large black and white building with red brickwork.

This has had a chequered history, having been at different times: a private stand for the local racecourse; a gentleman's residence (although changing hands many times); a hotel for 13 years from 1895; a convalescent home for railwaymen, over a period of 70 years. During the First World War it was used for housing German prisoners and later used as a temporary depository for records and papers of Wirral Councils. In 1982, it finally re-opened as a hotel.

The building itself is a mixture of architecture. The original octagonal tower was erected in 1593 by Ferdinando Stanley, 6th Earl of Derby, for watching his sporting activities including horse racing and hawking and the first Derby horse race was run here on the sands.

Turn around and go back to the end of the golf course. Turn left down the ramp and follow a concrete road to the main road ('Leasowe Road') and turn right. At the junction with 'Pasture Road', where the main road bends left, either turn left to the station or right into the car park to complete the walk.

Moreton & Wallasey

Pleasant walking along the embankment and beach.

Start: *Car park at the end of 'Pasture Road', Moreton.*
Grid ref: 258 915.

Distance: *6.5km/4 miles.*

Parking: *Car park at end of 'Pasture Road', Moreton or travel by train to Moreton Railway station, turn right out of station and walk to the car park.*

Refreshments: *Leasowe Castle Hotel, Brewer's Fayre (old Derby Pool Baths).*

Points of Interest: *Leasowe Castle Hotel.*

The walk

From the car park go up onto the embankment, turn right and walk along it. After passing 'Leasowe Castle Hotel' you will come to a delightful sandy beach with sandhills behind. Continue walking until you see what looks like an old signpost indicating 'Leasowe 1 mile to right, New Brighton 2 miles straight ahead'.

The signpost is not old at all, having been designed in 1998 for the National Cycle Network and is their Route 56.

Continue on towards New Brighton and soon you will see the site of the old Derby Pool on your right.

This was the first swimming pool to be opened in Wallasey in 1932 and could accommodate 1000 bathers. It closed in 1978 and is now a Brewer's Fayre establishment where you can obtain food and drinks.

Retrace your steps back to the car park or railway station at Moreton.

(For a shorter walk of 4km or 2½ miles, walk just in the one direction, then continue from the Brewer's Fayre pub up the road. Turn right into 'Bayswater Road' then left into 'Harrison Drive' and you will soon come to 'Grove Road' railway station on your right. From here you can catch a train to Birkenhead North then change for Moreton on the West Kirby line.)

Leasowe Castle Hotel

Hoylake

This walk leads down to the sea front in Hoylake then along the beach to West Kirby with it's wide views out over the River Dee to Hilbre Island and North Wales. It may not be possible to walk the beach at high tide when an inland option is available.

Start: *Hoylake railway station. Grid ref: 217 888.*

Distance: *5.5km/3½ miles.*

Parking: *By Hoylake railway station where there is a large (paying) car park, or come by train.*

Refreshments: *The 'Green Lodge' does a Sunday Carvery.*

Points of Interest: *The King's Gap; Hilbre Islands; Red Rocks; Hoylake Lighthouse; Royal Liverpool Golf Club.*

The walk

From the station car park turn left andwalk to the roundabout. Cross the roundabout and continue ahead along the road ('The King's Gap').

On 12th August 1689, King William III set sail for Ireland from Hoylake with his troops to fight James II and his French allies, giving this road its unusual name. He was victorious at the Battle of the Boyne on 12th July 1690, the following year. In those days Hoylake was a thriving port with regular crossings to Ireland. However, if the wind was not favourable, potential travellers might have to wait several days at Hoylake for better conditions.

Continue walking along 'The Kings Gap' to the end, passing to the right of the 'Green Lodge Hotel'. At the promenade, turn left and walk along the beach to Red Rocks and the Lighthouse. If the tide is high you may not be able to do this, in which case

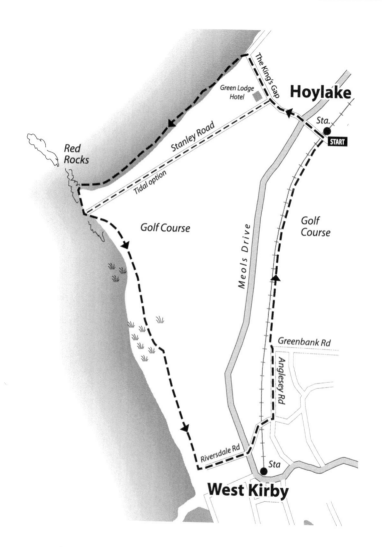

return to the 'Green Lodge Hotel' and turn right along 'Stanley Road'.

Ahead of you is Hilbre Island but do not attempt to walk out to the island from this point as it is extremely dangerous. It is possible to reach the islands from West Kirby by crossing over at certain times depending on the tide. Information about this can be found on the notice board at the end of Dee Lane in West Kirby.

From Red Rocks, walk left along the beach to West Kirby keeping to the left of the marsh grass, now a nature reserve and home to the natterjack toad which is a protected species. The sand is quite firm and dry here.

At West Kirby, go up the steps and turn left up 'Riversdale Road' to the end. Cross the main road and, going to the right of the United Reformed Church, proceed up 'Bridge Road' which crosses the railway. Take the first road on your left ('Orrysdale'/'Anglesey Road') and follow the road, passing a school. As the road bends right you will see a sign for a combined footpath and cycle path. Turn left on to this path and follow it beside the railway all the way back to Hoylake station to complete the walk.

Looking across to Hilbre from Red Rocks

WALK 4

Meols

This walk follows the promenade from Meols to 'The King's Gap' in Hoylake, then returns by lanes and field paths to Meols.

Start: *Junction of 'Meols Parade' and 'Dovepoint Road'. Grid ref: 231 906 (or Meols railway station, grid ref: 234 898).*

Distance: *7.5km/4¾ miles.*

Parking: *Cars can be parked on the sea front at the end of 'Dovepoint Road', Meols.*

Public Transport: *Meols railway station.*

Refreshments: The *'Green Lodge' at 'The King's Gap', Hoylake.*

Points of Interest: *The King's Gap; The Bigger Plant Company.*

The walk

Turn left (when looking out to sea) and walk along the sea front passing the new life boat station to the 'The King's Gap' at Hoylake where the road turns left away from the beach.

Wirral Council allows sand yachting and paracarting on the beach at Hoylake but to take part you must be a member of Wirral Sand-yacht Club. From here a wreck can sometimes be seen to the north of Hilbre Island at low water. This is the remains of the 'Nestos', a Greek cargo ship, which sank in 1971 on its way to Seaforth Dock from New Orleans with a cargo of Sulphur.

Follow the road left away from the beach and walk along to the 'Green Lodge' pub.

On 12th August 1689, King William III set sail for Ireland from Hoylake with his troops to fight against James II and his French allies, hence the name 'The King's Gap'. He was victorious at the Battle of the Boyne on 12th July 1690, the following year.

Continue ahead to the roundabout, then go straight ahead to Hoylake railway station. Cross the level crossing and follow 'Carr Lane' round to the left. At 'New Hall Lane', turn right and walk down the lane between small industrial units.

After 'New Hall Farm' the lane becomes a track, crosses the golf course, bends right, then bends left. Look for a wooden footbridge and stile on your left in about 200 yards. Cross the bridge and stile and proceed ahead along the edge of the field and over another stile and footbridge. Continue on across three fields and over a stile. Follow the footpath ahead and look for a stile on your right where overhead power lines branch right. Cross this stile and follow the path ahead which eventually

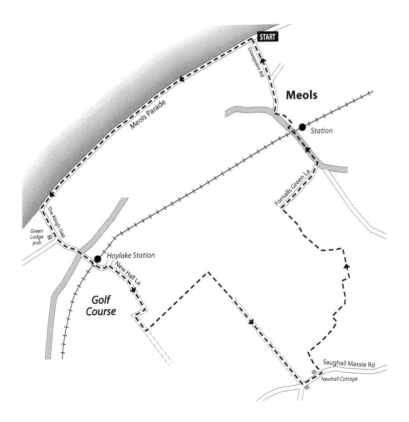

Walking along Meols Parade

becomes a farm track and a tarmac road. Continue to the main road opposite 'China Farm Lane'.

Turn left and walk along the road, taking care as there is no pavement. After 'Newton Hall Cottage', (a modern bungalow), turn left and follow a farm track through fields (footpath no.7).

Follow the track as it turns right and at end of the track go straight across the field to the opposite hedge. Turn left in front of the hedge and follow the path to where the signed footpath goes through a gap in the hedge on the right. Go through the gap and continue ahead along the left-hand side of the following field to a stile and footbridge in the corner. Continue ahead along the field edge to a stile on your left. Cross the stile and another one opposite, then walk straight ahead through the field. About half way across, turn right by two straining posts and continue in a straight line to the edge of the field. Turn left along a concrete track and at a T junction at the end of the track, turn left again. Continue to a stile in the next field boundary on your right. Follow the path along the side of the field with the hedge on your right.

Cross a stile in the corner and go straight across the following field bearing right along a track. Turn left over a small bridge by a farm, then immediately right into 'Fornall's Green Lane'. Continue along this lane, passing The Bigger Plant Company to arrive at the main road.

The Bigger Plant Company supplied the golfing tree sculptures at stations in 2006, during and after the Open Golf Championship when the competition came to Hoylake.

Turn left, cross the road and walk over the bridge passing Meols railway station which could be used as an alternative start. Pass a line of shops and take the second road on the right ('Dovepoint Road') to reach the sea front and complete the walk.

West Kirby

This walk takes in West Kirby promenade with its marine lake and a section along the beach. Inland it follows the Wirral Way then heads through the old village onto the hill. There are options to visit St. Bridget's church and the Dawson Brown archaeological museum (by prior arrangement) before continuing through Ashton Park with its rose gardens, lake and wildlife.

A good family walk with lots for children to see and do and plenty of suitable picnic spots.

Start: *At the end of 'Dee Lane' by the sailing centre and promenade. Grid ref: 210 868.*

Distance: *5.5km/3½ miles.*

Parking: *Parking is available on the Promenade at the end of 'Dee Lane' or in the nearby car park (paying).*

Public transport: *West Kirby railway station.*

Refreshments: *Numerous cafés, bars and restaurants in the centre of West Kirby.*

Points of Interest: *St. Bridget's Church (open Mon-Fri. and Sun afternoons in summer), Charles Dawson Brown Museum in the old school next to the church. Contact: Rod Tann 0151 625 1234 for admission.*

The walk

From the sailing centre at the end of 'Dee Lane' and opposite the car park, either walk along the promenade or follow the path around the Marine Lake, (sometimes a bit wet underfoot!).

On reaching the 'West Kirby Sailing Club' at the end of the promenade (or the lake), go right and walk along the beach. After the sailing club there are houses and gardens up to the left. Continue along the beach and turn left up the second contructed pathway in about 500 yards. At the top of the bank you can sit and admire the view across the Dee estuary to Wales. This is a good place for a picnic.

Follow the gravel path to the Wirral Way and turn left. Follow the path along the old trackbed to the first bridge over. Turn right up the steps immediately before the bridge and at the top turn left then right along the main road ('Sandy Lane') to the newsagents ('Bridge House Stores'). Cross the road here and walk along 'Ludlow Drive' to the Charles Dawson Brown Museum and church on your left.

The museum is only open by special arrangement (for admission, contact Rod Tann on: 0151 625 1234). Charles Dawson Brown was

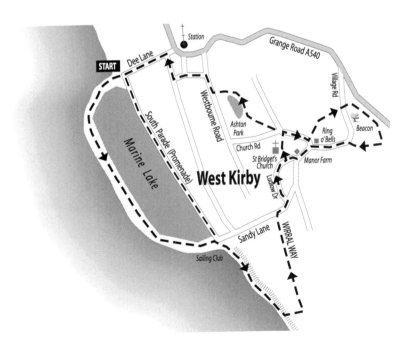

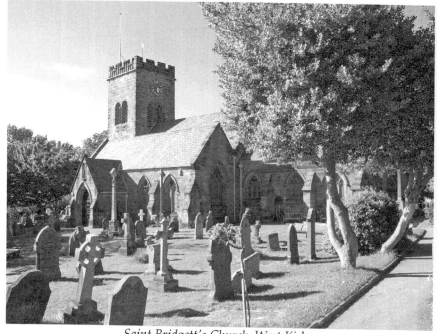

Saint Bridgett's Church, West Kirby

born in West Kirby in 1830 and was a keen historian. When he died in 1890, his collection of ancient crosses and other relics were housed in the old school house next to the church and named the Charles Dawson Brown Museum. It was opened in 1892. The church has some very fine stained glass windows and an old hog's back tombstone.

Walk through the churchyard and leave by the lychgate. If you wish to shorten the walk, cross the road after leaving the church and walk through Ashton Park – see ***below, otherwise turn right along 'Rectory Road'.

After passing 'The Rectory' on your right, turn left up a path on the bend of the lane. Walk up this path to the road, cross over and climb up the steps to the beacon on top of the hill.

There is a fine view from here across the Dee estuary to the Welsh hills and along the North Wales coast to the Great Orme. The Beacon was originally used as a landmark by shipping.

Turn right at the top of the steps (with the Beacon in front of you) and follow a good path until you come to a narrow intersecting path in a slight dip. Turn right here and walk downhill. At the bottom turn right along 'Wetstone Lane' then left at the end into 'Village Road'. Walk down the road passing the restaurant (previously the 'Ring O' Bells' pub) and 'Manor Farm' (an old farmhouse circa 1655). A little further on turn right along 'St Bridget's Lane', then right towards the church again, but this time walk along the footpath to the right of the churchyard. Note the uneven ground on your right in the field

Wreckers and smugglers are said to have operated in Wirral in the past and when bodies were found on the beach, they were brought up Church Road, or 'Corpse Lane' as it was called, on carts to the church and it is believed that they were buried in this field. Hopefully the field will be excavated when funds become available.

***Cross the road, enter 'Ashton Park' and follow the tree-lined pathway across the 'Milennium Rose Garden'. At the end of the path cross over the bridge to the lake and turn right.

On Saturday and Sunday afternoons in summer you can obtain a welcome cup of tea at the hut by the bowling green.

Walk beside the lake passing a children's playground on the right. Leave the park to the left of the playground and walk out to the road. Turn right along the road and turn left into 'North Road' opposite the Methodist Church. Turn right into 'Banks Road', then left into 'Dee Lane' and follow this down to the Promenade to complete the walk.

Grange

A good walk for access by public transport, linking Hoylake and West Kirby railway stations and taking in a nature reserve on the way.

Start: *West Kirby railway station. Grid ref: 213 869.*

Distance: *5.25km/3¼ miles.*

Parking: *Car Park on the corner of 'Dee Lane' (paying) near the sailing centre or behind the Concourse.*

Refreshments: *Numerous cafés around 'Banks Road' and the railway station area, or picnic by the Nature Reserve.*

Points of Interest: *War Memorial; Gilroy Nature Reserve.*

The walk

From West Kirby railway station, turn left and walk past the Concourse and up 'Grange Road'. Turn left into 'Gerard Road' and walk to the end. Take the footpath which continues ahead, then bears right to the top of Grange Hill and the War Memorial with magnificent views of Hilbre Islands, West Kirby and Hoylake, the estuaries of the River Dee and River Mersey, Liverpool and the Lancashire coast.

Every year a Remembrance Day service is held here in what is a small amphitheatre in front of the memorial column.

Take one of the paths which heads north from the memorial (towards the windfarms on the skyline). This will bring you to a road with housing opposite ('Lang Lane'). Turn right and at the end of the road enter the cemetery. Go ahead along the road, then cross over the playing field on your left to 'Somerset Road', passing a block of flats. Turn left at a T junction, then cross over and turn right into 'Gilroy Road' by 'Coronation Buildings'. Take the first path on the left through a gate and along a tarmac bridleway to 'Gilroy Nature Reserve', created by local residents. Turn left and follow the footpath around the pond.

Turn left to rejoin the tarmac path again and continue to the end into 'Newhall Lane' by 'Newhall Farm'. At the end of the lane, turn left and follow the road round to Hoylake railway station where you can catch a train back to West Kirby. If you wish you can return to West Kirby (an extra mile) along the footpath to the left immediately before the level crossing. At the end continue along 'Anglesey Road'. Cross over 'Bridge Road' and go straight ahead back to the Concourse and railway station on your right.

Rock Ferry

A short urban walk along the River Mersey.

Start: *'The Admiral', Rock Ferry. (To reach the pub go down 'Rock Lane East' over the A41 bypass.) Grid ref: 335 868.*

Distance: *1.5km/1 mile.*

Parking: *By 'The Admiral' pub (now closed).*

Refreshments: *None available.*

Points of Interest: *Pier and slipway; shore and esplanade; houses in Rock Park.*

The walk

Walk from the pub to the slipway and turn right along the waterfront.

The pier was built in 1897. The slipway was built in 1805 and was the first to be built on the River Mersey. There has been talk for many years of improving the waterfront along to Eastham but nothing seems to have come of the talks so far.

A short distance along the waterfront was the site of the old public baths which were only demolished in recent years and is now the site of a block of flats. As you look across the river to Liverpool you will see the Anglican Cathedral with the Roman Catholic Cathedral just behind it to the left.

Walk to the end of the esplanade where you will see in front of you the site of what was New Ferry Pier (a small rounded promontory to the left of a grassy area.) *The mud flats below the esplanade have been declared a Site of Special Scientific Interest (SSSI) by English Nature. It is the feeding ground for pintail ducks and black-tailed godwits.*

Looking acros to the Liverpool skyline

Turn right just before the site of New Ferry Pier and return along the path next to 'Rock Park Road'. Join 'Rock Park Road' and turn right in front of the very fine houses of Rock Park. Go through iron gates and continue along the road. *On your left you will notice a subway under the bypass. This has been decorated with paintings by local children.* Continue walking to the end of Rock Park then turn left up the road and after passing the bypass turn left again where you will find the gatepost of No. 26, Hawthorn House, where Nathaniel Hawthorne lived.

Nathaniel Hawthorne was a famous American author who became a consul in Liverpool in the mid 19th century (1853-57) and made his home in Rock Park, along with other wealthy and famous people of his day. Sadly, his house was one of the ones demolished when the bypass was built and now only one of the gate posts is still standing in his memory.

Retrace your steps to finish at 'The Admiral' pub.

Bidston

A walk across Bidston Hill to Bidston village and back to Tam O'Shanter Cottage and Urban Farm. The farm has various farm animals and some rare breeds and is a child's paradise! Throughout the summer months there are numerous events and activities organised by the rangers. Telephone the ranger on: 0151 653 9332 for information on the farm and Bidston Hill.

Start: *Car park by Tam O'Shanter Farm. Grid ref: 291 894.*

Distance: *3km/1¾ miles.*

Parking: *Tam O'Shanter car park.*

Refreshments: *Tam O'Shanter Café – open 7 days a week 9.30am to 4.30pm.*

Points of Interest: *Windmill and observatory; old stone carving and packhorse trail; Bidston Hall and village.*

The walk

Leave the car park in the left-hand corner (use the map and information board as a reference) and follow the footpath signed to 'Windmill ¼m' across the open green area. Bear right at a fork as you enter woods and head towards the windmill when it comes into view, crossing the road ('Vyner Road North') via the footbridge.

There has been a mill on this site since about 1590 and at 70.4 metres or 231feet, it is one of Wirral's highest points. This mill dates from 1800 and finished working in 1875.

Keep to the left of the mill, following the path ahead along the ridge to the observatory and lighthouse beyond it.

There are good views of Liverpool to your right.

Pass to the left of the observatory and the lighthouse and continue until you reach a large flat stone slab. *This contains the ancient carving of a horse (eroded but still visible) which faces exactly towards the midsummer sunrise (head faces left). There are also the remains of an old packhorse trail, recently discovered to the left side of the stone slab.*

Beyond the slab follow the path ahead then leftwards down beside a sandstone wall on the left to join an access track with houses on the left. Follow this track down to a T junction. Turn right and pass Bidston Hall on your right with its beautiful ornamental wrought iron gates.

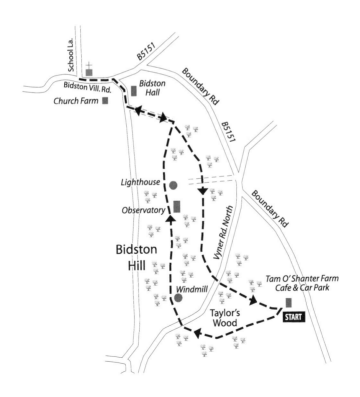

This is one of the oldest Halls in Wirral, built around 1580 by the 6th Earl of Derby. Turn left into Bidston village with its many old sandstone buildings. *Note in particular 'Church Farm', built in the 17th century with many different floor levels! A small cenotaph has the names of local men killed in action during World War I, plus a nurse killed whilst administering to the wounded.*

Retrace your steps past Bidston Hall and turn left up the track back onto Bidston Hill.

At the flat sandstone slab with the carving, bear left where the path forks. Continue along below the new observatory, crossing over the access road. After crossing the road, bear left where the path forks and continue until you reach a broken stone wall on your left. Walk ahead a few more yards to a crossing path, turn left and head for the road.

Cross the road and go through Taylor's Wood via FP25 (opposite and a little to the left) to return to the car park.

The windmill on Bidston Hill

Looking across to Little Eye, Hilbre Island, from West Kirby (walk 3)

Walking around the Marine Lake, West Kirby (walk 5)

Black and white architecture and the fine Norman style church at Thornton Hough (walk 20)

Hill Bark, Royden Park (walk 10)

The fine lowland heath at Thurstaston Common (walk 10)

*Following gentle field paths between Brimstage and Thornton Hough
(walk 19)*

On Thurstaston Hill with wide views to the Welsh hills (walk 10)

The 'Wheatsheaf Inn', Raby (walk 23)

Walking through Dibbinsdale Local Nature Reserve (walk 22)

Walking along the old seafront, Parkgate (walk 25)

Denhall Quay, Little Neston (walk 26)

Fountain, Port Sunlight (walk 21)

WALK 9

Tranmere

An urban walk linking two of the town's Victorian parks.

Start: *By the allotments opposite Mersey Park Primary School in Elm Road. Grid ref: 319 873.*

Distance: *3.25km/2 miles.*

Parking: *Car park by Mersey Park Primary School or roadside.*

Refreshments: *Picnic in the park as pubs don't serve food and there are no cafes nearby.*

Points of interest: *Allotments, site of Tranmere Hall, Tranmere Cross.*

The walk

From the car park, cross the road to look at the allotments.

These were renovated in 2003 by a local partnership initiative to encourage people in the area to use them, both as a means of healthy exercise and production of cheap, wholesome food. Pupils from the local schools attended the opening ceremony and pupils from Rock Ferry High School helped with the renovation.

Pass the school and enter Mersey Park. Walk down the right-hand side path and around the perimeter, returning to the gateway in 'Elm Road'.

The park covers an area of 21 acres and was opened in 1885. In the 1950s, the launching of the Ark Royal at Cammell Laird's shipyard was watched from here by the pupils of Mersey Park Primary School.

Turn right along 'Agnes Road' and at the end pass between the fine pillars marking an entrance to the park, with Mersey Lodge in front of you and Carlton Mount to your left.

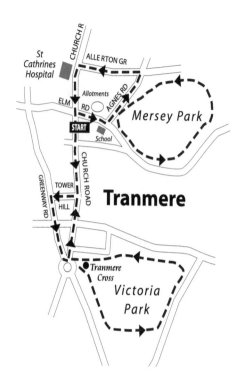

Notice the fine three-storey red brick houses from a time when this area was obviously more affluent and fashionable than it is today.

Continue left into 'Allerton Grove' and 'Church Road' where you will see the church like an oasis on the edge of the grounds of St Catherine's Hospital.

This hospital was a workhouse in the 19th century.

Continue along 'Church Road', passing 'Walker Street' and 'Dial Road' then proceed right, up 'Tower Hill'. Look back at the wonderful view across the River Mersey.

Turn left along 'Greenway Road' to the roundabout.

Tower Hill runs through the middle of what was the 1½ acre estate of Tranmere Hall which had frontages on 'Church Road' (approx. numbers 108 -134) and to 'Greenway Road' (approx. numbers 69-91) and bounded by 'Dial Road'. As you walk along 'Greenway Road', note the difference in roof height and architecture between numbers 91 and 93. The houses on your right were built in the middle to late 1930s and are known as the Tranmere Hall Estate.

At the roundabout, cross the road and enter Victoria Park, built in 1901 and covering an area of 29 acres.

In front of you is Tranmere Cross, dating from about 1500AD.

Turn right and follow the path, passing the bowling green and an ugly block of flats which, relatively recently, replaced a beautiful old mansion called 'The Towers'. Continue round the perimeter path. Leave the park and turn right along 'Church Road'.

At the top of 'Well Lane' (on the right), there used to be three blocks of back-to-back houses which were only demolished in the 1960s.

Continue walking along 'Church Road' until you reach 'Elm Road' and the car park.

In the 1840s, Tranmere comprised six farms, several large private dwellings, a pinfold (destroyed in 1935), two quarries, a small brewery, three ale houses, two shops, at least 50 cottages and an ancient cross. Walker Street and Walker Place were named after a Mr W.W. Walker who owned the quarry there. The inns were located near the crossroads of the village centre. One was the Black Horse Inn *near the top of Well Lane and dated 1757. The* Sportsman's Arms *at the top of Prenton Road East was a small whitewashed, thatched building until the 1930s. The third inn was* The Hare *in Church Road near the corner of Tower Road. It was demolished at the end of the 19th century. In the 1830s and 1840s a large part of Tranmere Hall was let as lodgings to summer visitors! (hard to imagine holiday makers in Tranmere).*

Also in the 1800s, Thomas Brassey built a new turnpike road from Tranmere to Chester. It was called New Chester Road—the present A41, beyond the bottom of Mersey Park.

Frankby

A walk through the woods of Royden Park and up over Thurstaston Hill where there are magnificent views across northern Wirral to the Lancashire coast and west over the River Dee to North Wales. A return is made through farmland.

Start: *Royden Park. Grid ref: 246 857 (or the 'Farmer's Arms', Frankby, grid ref: 246 863).*

Distance: *6.5km/4 miles.*

Parking: *Public car park in Royden Park.*

Refreshments: *The 'Farmers Arms', Frankby or 'The Cottage Loaf' at Thurstaston.*

Points of Interest: *Hillbark.*

The walk

From the car park by the WC block walk back to the driveway and turn left towards 'Hillbark'. Turn left along a narrow footpath just before the main entrance, signed 'Thurstaston Common', keeping 'Hillbark' on your right. Pass two open grass areas on your left until you come to a sandstone wall. Pass the wall into Thurstaston Common and continue straight ahead on a good path.

At the end of the path a large gate leads onto a sandy track. Follow the track past 'Benty Farm' and in 100 yards or so, where the track bears left take the path straight ahead under power cables. This path leads through woods to a lane end at a kissing gate. Go through the gate and take the path which bears right with a steady climb to the top of the hill, marked by a triangulation pillar and a viewfinder.

There are magnificent views from here across the River Dee to the Flintshire coast and the hills of North Wales.

Facing the River Dee, head left from the summit and follow one of the sandy paths down to a car park on the main road.

To your left along the road is 'The Cottage Loaf'—a good place to stop—otherwise turn right out of the car park, cross over and walk along the main road. After the rock cutting there is a sandstone wall. At the end of the wall turn left through a gap and follow the signed path down across the heath (National Trust) to a gate. Go through a gap at the side of the gate and pass in front of houses to return to the main road.

Turn left here through a kissing gate on to footpath 15. In the far corner go through another kissing gate and go ahead between paddocks to an access track. Follow the track ahead to the road. Turn

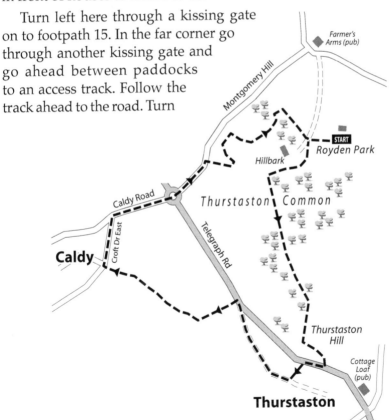

Thurstaston Common

right here ('Croft Drive East'), then right again at the T junction and walk along to Caldy Cross Roads and a roundabout.

Cross the busy road with care and continue straight on until you come to footpath 13 on your right. Turn right and follow this path. Go through a kissing gate and follow the path with a metal fence on your right. Turn left at a 'National Trust' sign and go through a gap in the wall. Turn left along the wall, then bear right and walk beside a wooden fence.

Go straight ahead at a clearing, soon walking beside the fence on the left and close to the road, not visible but within earshot. Continue until you reach a broad path and turn right to return to the car park.

WALK 11

Greasby

An easy walk mainly on field paths well supplied with stiles and kissing gates and tracks around the old RAF airfield.

Start: *Greasby Library. Grid ref: 254 873.*

Distance: *5.25km/3¼ miles.*

Parking: *Park by the library in the centre of Greasby (access via bypass).*

Refreshments: *Pubs in Greasby village or take a picnic and eat it by the lake.*

Points of Interest: *Village pump; RAF memorial.*

The walk

Leave the library car park, cross the bypass using the pedestrian crossing and turn left to the roundabout where you will find the restored village pump.

Turn right and walk down 'Pump Lane' to the end of the houses on your left. Turn left into 'Ashdale Park' and bear right onto footpath number 56 behind bungalows. Follow the path over a footbridge and through a kissing gate and across two fields, to bring you to a second footbridge and kissing gate. Follow the signed path 'FP9 to Grange' ahead across the field to arrive at another kissing gate. Cross a track and go ahead through another kissing gate, into a copse. Follow the footpath ahead to reach a track (one of the old concrete roads of the airfield) and turn right. Turn left at the T junction and follow track to the road.

Here you will find a memorial to commemorate all those who served, trained and worked at RAF West Kirby between 1940 and 1957.

Cross the road and follow 'Oldfield Lane'. Just before 'Oldfield

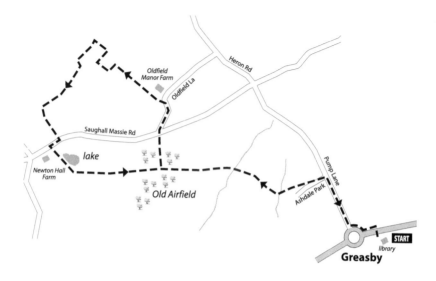

Manor Farm', take the footpath for 'Meols' to the left of the garden.

This footpath has been adopted by the RA Wirral under the Local Paths Partnership between Wirral Met. Borough and the Countryside Commission Joint Initiative. For further details telephone: 051 643 7098.

Continue along this path ignoring the first stile on the left, then around the edge of the field to the corner where you will find another stile on your left. Cross this stile and walk straight ahead to a gap in the hedge in the corner. Go through the gap and turn left along the edge of the field. In about 50 yards turn right across the field to meet a track. Follow this track ahead to the road (FP7).

Turn right, cross the road and climb over a stile (FP9) opposite a bungalow. Follow the footpath straight ahead between hedges with a small lake over the hedge to the left and over a second stile. At the end of the path turn left over a stile and walk beside the lake.

Cross the stile in the corner, then head straight across the following field to another stile in the far hedge. Cross this stile and follow the path through woodland, crossing over two tracks to return to the kissing gate crossed earlier in the walk. Retrace your outward route across the fields and back to Greasby.

RAF Memorial

WALK 12

Newton & Larton

An easy pleasant walk along field paths and quiet lanes.

Start: *'The Ridger' pub. Grid ref: 234 868.*

Distance: *6km/3¾ miles.*

Parking: *'The Ridger' if you are using the pub or in the road.*

Refreshments: *Excellent food in the pub served all day Mon. to Sat. 12 – 8.30pm Sunday 12 – 4pm. A suitable place for families as there is a garden to play in and lots of seats and tables outside if the weather is fine.*

Points of Interest: *Paddock burial ground; Royden Manor; old cottages.*

The walk

From 'The Ridger', go left along 'Frankby Road' out of Newton towards Frankby. Pass 'Bay Tree Road' on the right in Frankby

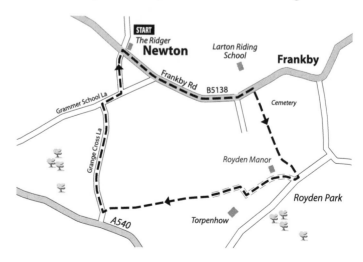

42

The Ridger

and oposite 'Larton Riding School', turn right on the footpath signed to 'Thurstaston'.

At the end of the path, turn right along a rough access road signed to 'Caldy'.

On your right is a paddock which is reputed to be an old graveyard and beside it is Royden Manor with its ornate gate posts.

Continue to 'Torpenhow', the large house beyond the wall-enclosed gardens where the track becomes a footpath. *This used to be a school for children with special needs but has now been converted to flats.* Follow the path right around the gardens beside the wall.

Cross an old stone stile at the end of the path and walk down the right edge of the following field to a footbridge. This leads onto a path between gardens. Turn right at the road and follow it to the old sandstone cottages just before the shops.

Turn right here and follow the road, which soon bends left, back to 'The Ridger' to complete the walk.

WALK 13

Irby

An enjoyable walk through National Trust woodland and along the edge of Thurstaston Common. In addition there is Limbo Lane Plantation and Harrock Wood so if you like woodland walking, this is a walk for you.

Start: *The 'Anchor Inn' pub, Irby. Grid ref: 256 845.*

Distance: *6km/3¾ miles.*

Parking: *Behind Irby Library.*

Refreshments: *The 'Anchor Inn' pub; 'Heatherlands Court'; 'Irby Mill' pub (half way around walk). 'The Shippons' (centre of Irby).*

Points of Interest: *Replica of village stocks by Library; Irby Hall; National Trust woodland.*

The walk

The walk begins from the footpath to the side of the 'Anchor Inn' but first walk along the road a short distance, passing the telephone box, to see Irby Hall.

Irby Hall is an example of a 16th century manor house but many of its historic features have been lost during renovation work. However parts of its moat still exist

Take the footpath across the field to left of the 'Anchor Inn'. Bear right at the end of the field over a stile and into 'Dawlish Road'. Go left to a signed path between houses and turn right on an enclosed path at the back of gardens. Cross a stile into fields at the end of the path, pass a pond and head for a gate beside a farmhouse. Follow the right of way between outbuildings and the house to reach the road.

Cross over, turn right and walk along the road to 'Heatherlands

The village stocks, Irby

Court' where you can have an excellent Sunday lunch, but you must book beforehand (tel: 0151 648 1807). You could start the walk here if you prefer as parking is available in their car park if having lunch or in nearby 'School Lane'.

Cross 'School Lane' and enter the National Trust area through a kissing gate ahead. Go ahead on the obvious path never far from the edge of the wood on your right. Ignore the right turn out of the woods by houses on the right (National Trust information board here), instead bear left and stay on the path still close to the edge of the woods.

At the end of the wood in a corner, turn right over a small footbridge and up steps. Go straight ahead now ignoring a path on the left to reach an access track between two cottages. Bear right along the track ahead away from the cottages and turn left at a junction past more cottages then bear right to the road. Turn left along the road to the roundabout by 'Irby Mill' pub. Turn

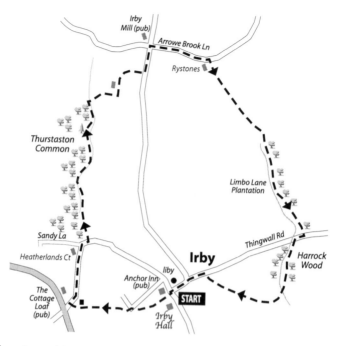

right along 'Arrowe Brook Lane'. The road is sometimes busy but there is a wide grass verge.

In about 400 yards turn right onto the signed footpath immediately after a house on the right ('Rystones'). Follow this path to 'Thingwall Road', ignoring a permissive path off to your left just before you enter woods.

At the road, turn right, cross over and enter Harrock Wood almost opposite. Follow the footpath through the trees and alongside Arrowe Brook. Continue to the end of the wood, then enter a field via a wooden kissing gate, turn right, cross the brook by stone steps and enter a field. Go ahead up the right-hand hedge line to cross a stile on the right which leads along a short access road into Irby village. Turn left and return to the Library.

Note the replica stocks by the Library. The original ones were put into storage in Birkenhead when the Library was being built but sadly they were 'lost'!

Arrowe Country Park

THIS *walk explores the woods and pathways bordering Arrowe Country Park, then uses field paths to reach Irby and a return to Arrowe Country Park.*

Start: *Arrowe Country Park car park. Grid ref: 265 869.*

Distance: *6km/3¾ miles.*

Parking: *Arrowe Country Park car park off Arrowe Brook Road by Arrowe Brook near Greasby.*

Refreshments: *Pubs nearby or in Greasby, but an excellent walk if you prefer a picnic.*

Arrowe Country Park

The walk

Leave the car park to right of the notice board following the tarmac path into the woods. Curve left with the path which then runs straight with the brook to the right.

In about 300 yards and shortly before the open grass area, bear right onto a narrow footpath. Follow this over a footbridge to a lake. Immediately before the lake there is a path junction. Turn right here through the trees and go through a kissing gate into fields. Turn right to the field corner, then go left up the field edge. Cross the stile in the corner and continue ahead to the road.

Turn left along the road until you come to a signed footpath on your left (immediately before 'Rystones'). Turn left and follow this path to 'Thingwall Road' on the edge of Irby.

Turn left along the road and after passing open fields on the left and 'Parkway', turn left into a small car parking area at the start of Footpath 27. Leave the car park through a kissing gate to the left of a bridle path and follow the path ahead through woods. At a boardwalk turn right, cross a footbridge and at a junction with a major path in about 30 yards turn left.

You are now walking along the edge of Arrowe Country Park. Keep to this path, eventually passing the lake again on the right. Retrace your steps back to the car park to complete the walk.

48

WALK 15

Woodchurch & Arrowe Park

A short easy walk exploring the woods of Arrowe Country Park, the countryside near Arrowe Park Hospital and the historic Woodchurch Parish Church.

Start: *Arrowe Country Park car park. Grid ref: 265 869.*

Distance: *3.5km/2¼ miles.*

Parking: *Arrowe Country Park car park off Arrowe Brook Road by Arrowe Brook near Greasby.*

Refreshments: *'Arrowe Park' or 'Cherry Orchard', (opposite Landican cemetery), which has an indoor and outdoor play area.*

Points of Interest: *Woodchurch Parish Church; Arrowe Hall.*

The walk

Leave the car park to right of the notice board following the tarmac path into the woods. Curve left with the path which then runs straight with the brook to the right. Shortly after the path opens out into a large grassed area take the gravel path on the left and walk towards the chimney of Arrowe Park Hospital. Pass the hospital and sports fields on the left to reach the main 'Arrowe Park Road' (Footpath 11).

Turn left, then cross the road at the crossing and walk down 'Pool Lane' opposite. After the bend follow the stone churchyard wall around to your right (opposite 'Meadow Crescent'). Turn right into 'Church Lane' to reach the church entrance. It is worth having a look around the churchyard and also the church if open.

Originally the school was in the churchyard but in 1873 the school and master's house were erected in their present position. In 1525, James

Goodacre left money to buy 20 yolk of oxen, later replaced with cows, to hire out to the poor people of the parish. A bread charity was started by William Gleave in 1646 and added to by other people's bequests. The bread was usually distributed at Eastertime.

From the churchyard go ahead along 'Church Lane' past 'The Rectory' and the school, then bear right along the road to the traffic lights. After passing the 'Arrowe Park' hotel (a good stop for a drink or meal), cross the road and enter Arrowe Park through the impressive entrance directly ahead.

Arrowe Park was given to the citizens of Birkenhead for leisure use and was the scene of the World Scout Jamboree in 1929.

Follow main path up through the park passing Arrowe Hall on your right. Take the next turning right before a children's playground and right again continuing on into a wooded area.

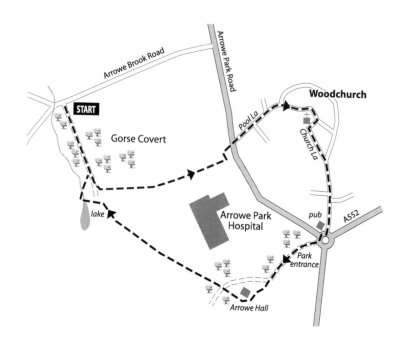

Arrowe Hall

Go over a footbridge and pass another play area with an aerial swing. Walk around this area and enter woods again.

At the first junction turn left and the path soon opens out into a large grass area with the hospital on your right. Continue along this path and when you are about 100 yards before the woods ahead, cross the grass on your left and follow the footpath over a bridge and waterfall. Turn right and follow the path over another bridge. Keep straight on then bear left onto the main path and return to the car park.

Thurstaston

AN interesting walk with wide views from the elevated path to Heswall, before a descent through the sandstone gorge of The Dungeon to join the Wirral Way. There are options to visit Thurstaston Visitor Centre and the beach before a return to the car park.

Start: *Thurstaston Church. Grid ref: 247 842.*

Distance: *5.5km/3½ miles.*

Parking: *Small layby opposite Thurstaston Church.*

Refreshments: *'Cottage Loaf' pub on A540; Church Farm shop and cafe (closes at 5 pm).*

Points of Interest: *Church Farm Organics—organic farm shop and tearooms; The Dungeon; Thurstaston Visitor Centre in Wirral Country Park (tel: 0151 648 4371/3884).*

The walk

From green facing the church go left along the lane and on the bend follow the farm track ahead signed to 'Heswall' (go left to visit Church Farm shop – open 10am to 5pm). At the end of the farm track cross the stile and follow the enclosed footpath ahead between fields.

There are excellent views across the River Dee to North Wales from this footpath.

Eventually you reach a junction by woods on the right and a stream. Turn right and follow the footpath FP43 signed to the 'Wirral Way'. This takes you by the stream to The Dungeon ravine—a local beauty spot in a dell with a small waterfall—caused by a geological fault.

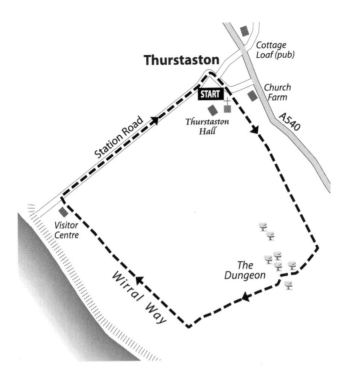

The path descends through the trees to a footbridge at the bottom of the slope. Cross the stream, turn right and continue along the path to the Wirral Way.

Turn right and walk along the Wirral Way, passing under the 'Dungeon Bridge' with another wonderful view across the Dee to North Wales. Keep to the left of metal gates to Thurstaston Visitor Centre with picnic areas and exhibitions and a pond for fishing. The Visitor Centre is open daily 10am to 5pm. Steps lead down to the beach if you have the time and energy.

Beyond the Visitor Centre turn right along 'Station Road'. Walk up road to the end and bear right back to the church to complete the walk.

To the right of Thurstaston Church is the historic Thurstaston Hall.

Landican

This walk links two of Wirral's ancient villages and follows part of the National Cycle Network.

Start: *Centre of Landican village by Home Farm. Grid ref: 283 857.*

Distance: *5.5km/3½ miles.*

Parking: *In centre of Landican opposite Home Farm.*

Refreshments: *'Cherry Tree' pub opposite Landican Cemetry is excellent for children, with a playground outside and a ball pond indoors.*

Points of interest: *The modern milestone in Storeton village.*

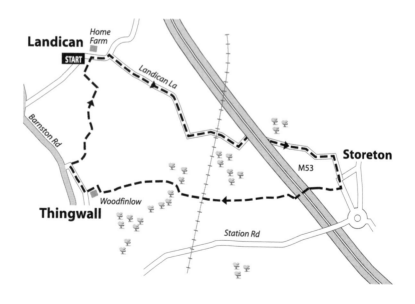

Landican

The walk

Leave the village in an easterly direction (right) then turn right onto the signed bridleway to 'Storeton'. This section follows part of cycle route 56 of the National Cycle Network. The route is obvious and is contained between hedges. The path eventually passes under the railway and the motorway.

On reaching Storeton village look for the new, ornate mile post on your right, indicating 'Landican 1½ miles'. You are nearly half way round your walk. This milepost is one of a thousand created for the millennium and creation of the National Cycle Network. It was funded by The Royal Bank of Scotland.

Just past the mile post, turn right over a stile and cross the field diagonally right. Cross motorway via a footbridge and head half-right across the following field. A wooden footbridge leads over a stream and the path continues ahead over another field, under electric pylons. Cross the railway with care and continue ahead through woodland. Go down wooden steps and over a footbridge and stile. Climb up the following field with a wooded pond on your right. Immediately after this bear half-right to go through a large field gate. Continue up the field beside the hedge crossing two stiles. This leads onto a narrow shrub-lined path. Follow the path to a track which turns left and passes stables.

At a house ('Woodfinlow Cottage'), turn right and follow the lane to 'Greenways Nurseries'. Cross a stile beside a gate and in 30 yards or so turn right through a caravan storage area. At the next large gate turn left onto a path and through two kissing gates by a pretty little wooden cottage on the right. Walk beside the fence on your left to a stile and footbridge in the corner, then go straight ahead through a large field with a hedge on your left until you come to a farm track. Turn left along the track and follow it as it bears right back to Landican village.

Landican

WALK 18

Storeton

An easy pleasant walk on good footpaths across fields and through woodland.

Start: *Centre of Storeton. Grid ref: 304 845.*

Distance: *4.5km/2¾ miles.*

Parking: *In the centre of the village or in a small layby almost opposite 'Rest Hill Road'.*

Refreshments: *'Traveller's Rest' pub, just off the route at the top of 'Rest Hill Road'.*

Points of Interest: *Storeton Quarry; Wirral Horn.*

The walk

From the parking area, take the public footpath (a farm track) signed to 'Brimstage'.

Over to your left you will see the rise up to Storeton Woods and the TV mast.

Pass a farm on the right, then go through a kising gate and ahead across a field towards the motorway. Cross a stile and walk parallel with the motorway to arrive in 'Brimstage Lane'.

Turn left by 'Ivy Boarding Kennels and Cattery' and walk along the lane. At a bend, turn right over a stile and take the path ahead across three fields towards Higher Bebington.

After the final stile turn left along a short lane then right up 'Red Hill Road'. Almost immediately, turn left onto the signed 'Public Footpath to Rest Hill Road' (FP 59), immediately to the left of a driveway. Follow the enclosed footpath beside two houses and gardens to join a track below the woods of Storeton Hill. Turn left along the track and continue to the road ('Rest Hill Road').

Cross over (or turn right here to visit the 'Traveller's Rest' pub) and enter Storeton Woods (Woodland Trust) ahead.

In 1838 footprints of the dinosaur, Cheirotherium where found in this area when it was a quarry. These can be seen in the Williamson Art Gallery in Birkenhead.

A tramway was opened in 1838 using second-hand rails from the Liverpool to Manchester railway. This transported the quarried sandstone to Bromborough Pool for shipment. The tramway was closed in 1905 and the north quarry was filled in with ½ million tons of earth taken from the first Mersey Tunnel when it was being excavated. Legend has it that a Roman soldier guards the quarry so keep your eyes open!

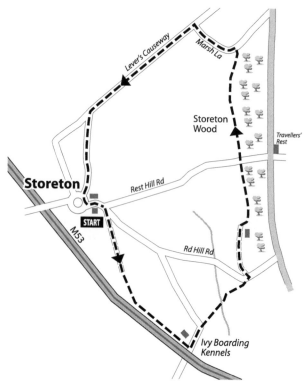

The village of Storeton

Through the trees you can see Storeton Hall Farm which contains remains of the old hall built by Sir William de Stanley in 1360. He was the Master Forester of Wirral and had as his symbol the Wirral Horn which is now in the possession of the Earl of Cromer's family who loaned it to Wirral Borough Council. It was displayed for about four months in 2007 at Wirral Museum. The horn may be returned to Wirral or a replica produced for display in Wirral Museum in Birkenhead.

Follow the straight path directly ahead through the woods until you come to 'Marsh Lane'. Turn left, follow this road to Lever Causeway and turn left again. At the roundabout turn left up 'Red Hill Road' and back to the centre of the village to complete the walk.

Brimstage

A short easy walk through farmland centered on the Brimstage Hall Craft Centre.

Start: *Brimstage Craft Centre, Brimstage. Grid ref: 304 827.*

Distance: *3km/1¾ miles.*

Parking: *Brimstage Craft Centre.*

Refreshments: *Country Mouse (for good home cooked lunches, coffee and cake and afternoon teas).*

Points of Interest: *Brimstage Hall — medieval tower is the oldest part; Craft Centre, small specialist shops and boutiques.*

Gentle field paths near Brimstage

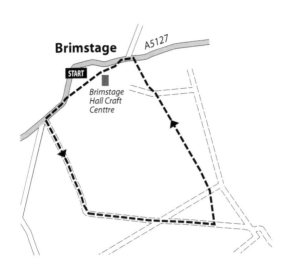

The walk

Climb over the stile at the back of the car park and take the field path ahead to the road. Go left along the road and left again into 'Talbot Avenue'. In a few yards turn left onto a signed bridleway (BR 47). At a junction just before a stile bear left. Continue to a private drive associated with nearby Thornton Manor. Cross over and continue along the bridleway opposite. At a footpath sign turn left and head directly across a field (if you reach a junction with a crossing track you have gone a little too far).

Cross over another drive and follow the path opposite. Walk ahead along field edges. *Look across fields to your left to see Brimstage Hall and its old tower.*

Cross a farm track by two stiles and keep ahead over one more field to reach Brimstage Road. Turn left along the road then left again into the Craft Centre.

This out-of-way village lies in the centre of Wirral and was originally the settlement of the Domville family, one of the most important families in Cheshire. In 1845, there were 135 people living here in 34 houses and there was one licensed place called the Red Cat. Compare that with today.

61

Thornton Hough

A short circular walk through level fields which could be combined with a stroll around the attractive village of Thornton Hough.

Start: *'The Seven Stars' pub in the village centre. Grid ref: 304 809.*

Distance: *4km/2½ miles.*

Parking: *Cars can parked in the centre of the village.*

Refreshments: *'The Seven Stars' pub, or excellent café in the Community Hall serving delicious home-made food.*

Points of Interest: *Two churches; Village Cross; Village Smithy.*

It is hard to believe that in 1847, a traveller described Thornton Hough as having 'a very unpleasant appearance, with the houses being of a very inferior description'. This changed between 1866 and 1877 when a retired woollen merchant named Joseph Hirst from Yorkshire came to live here. He built the parish church and school, the vicarage and a group of cottages and shops behind the church. Note his initials on 'The Store'. The church clock has five faces which enabled Joseph Hirst to see it from his bedroom window.

Later, Viscount Leverhulme bought Thornton Manor and built more houses similar to the ones he'd already built in Port Sunlight for his factory workers. He also built a school, a girls' orphanage, shops, a club and a village smithy complete with spreading chestnut tree (recently cut down sadly). No expense was spared when building the Congregational church (now United Reformed) which was commissioned by Viscount Leverhulme. It is pure Norman in style and unique in England.

Thornton Hough has won 'Best Kept Village' awards on several occasions and the huge village green is home to the Cricket Club.

The walk

Facing 'The Seven Stars', turn left along the main road until you come to a row of cottages on your left. Turn left beside the cottage onto a path which bears right by gardens to enter fields.

Walk along the field edge initially, then cut across the centre. Continue ahead beside the hedge in the following fields to a track. Turn left along the track which soon bears left to a junction with a crossing track. This is one of the private driveways associated with nearby Thornton Manor. Cross over and follow the footpath opposite (possibly an ancient trackway between the two banks).

Continue along this path, crossing over another driveway and following the path opposite. At a T-junction turn left and cross a stile into fields.

Thornton Manor, which can be seen over to the right, was transformed into an Elizabethan-style mansion by William Hesketh Lever, the first Viscount Leverhulm, who bought it in 1891.

Walk across the fields and cross the driveway again. The footpath opposite is well worn and heads directly through three fields to join an enclosed footpath. Follow this to yet another driveway. Turn right along the drive then left along a lane after the first house to return to the centre of Thornton Hough to complete the walk.

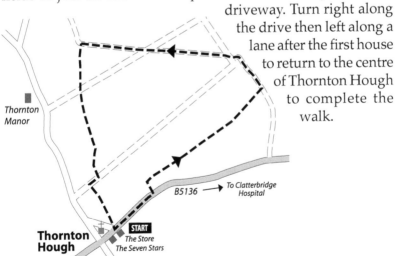

Thornton Manor

Thornton Hough

The Store

START
The Seven Stars

B5136 → To Clatterbridge Hospital

Port Sunlight

A short urban trail around the attractive village Port Sunlight. The walk is entirely on surfaced paths and roads and should take less than an hour. It is worth spending time, if you can, in the Sunlight Vision Centre (open until 4pm daily) and the Art Gallery which closes at 5pm.

Start: *Port Sunlight railway station. Grid ref: 337 840.*

Distance: *3km/1¾ miles.*

Parking: *Park near the station or come by train (Merseyrail) from Hamilton Square, Birkenhead.*

Refreshments: *'Sun Lounge Café' in the Garden Centre, and Lady Lever Art Gallery.*

Points of Interest: *War memorial; Lady Lever Art Gallery; Christ Church; The Lyceum; The Dell; Sunlight Vision Museum.*

The walk

Outside the railway station, look right and you will see 'Lever House', an impressive building from 1885 which contains the factory offices with the modern factory behind it. Originally, the factory had its own fire brigade of six men and a horse-drawn appliance. This was replaced in 1914 with a motor vehicle.

Close by on your right is the 'Gladstone Theatre', named after Prime Minister William Gladstone who opened it in 1891 as the men's dining hall. It was opened as a theatre in 1984 and has recently been refurbished.

Cross the road and turn left along 'Greendale Road' parallel to the railway. *Notice the genuine old paving slabs on the pavement.* Turn second right passing the garden centre (worth a visit for the 'Sun Lounge Café'). Continue on to the impressive nearby War Memorial.

This commemorates the lives of those villagers lost in World Wars I and II. This is quite a masterpiece and is the most significant War Memorial outside London.

Turn left at the memorial and walk down the rose-lined path, with seats, between 'Queen Mary's Drive' and 'King George's Drive' to the Art Gallery and Sunlight Vision Museum with displays on life in Port Sunlight in the late 1800s and early 1900s.

The Art Gallery is one of the finest in the country and houses many masterpieces by Constable, Turner, Millais, Rossetti and Ford Madox Brown as well as magnificent collections of Wedgewood china, beautifully carved and inlaid 18th century furniture, rich tapestries, ancient Greek urns, Roman statues and much more besides. It is open

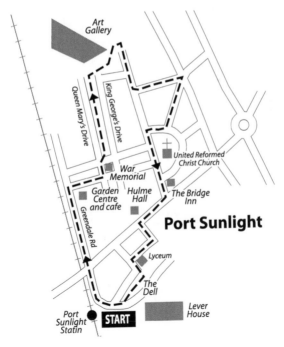

The impressive War Memorial in the centre of Port Sunlight

until 5pm each day. To the left of the Art Gallery is the impressive memorial to Lord Leverhulme erected in 1930 as a tribute from the workers.

Pass to the right of the Art Galley and bear right around the green area to a phone box. Turn left just after the phone box and walk down a tree-lined path.

Note the school on your right with its sunken playground built on land which was a tidal inlet from the River Mersey.

At the end of the path turn right, then right again on a footpath which brings you to the impressive United Reformed Christ Church.

Outside in the churchyard you will find the founder's tomb and those of other members of the Leverhulme family.

At one time there were as many as 600 children attending the Sunday School! There were so many that they had to be taught in eight different buildings.

Turn right and walk beside the churchyard to a T junction. Turn left here and walk beside the church to the end of the road by 'The Bridge Inn' so named because originally there was a bridge here across one of the tributaries of the Mersey. Turn right and walk along to Hulme Hall on the right.

Hulme was the maiden name of the first Viscount's wife. You can make a short detour here down the left-hand side of Hulme Hall to see the Memorial Garden to those who died in the Hillsborough Disaster in April 1989.

From Hulme Hall cross the road to look at the plaque on No. 20 Bolton Road. *King George V and Queen Mary made an unannounced visit in 1914 which must have caused quite a stir to the residents.*

Turn into 'Cross Street', walk around two sides of the bowling green and this will bring you to the Lyceum which now houses the Unilever Historical Archives. If shut, phone 0151 641 4551 to gain access or information. *On the opposite corner is 'Bridge Cottage' which was home to Leverhulme from 1896-7. It was also used for a scene in the film* 'Chariots of Fire' *in 1981.*

Turn left just after the Lyceum, cross the stone bridge beside 'Port Sunlight Village Social Club' and go down the steps on the left-hand side into The Dell.

This was originally another inlet from the River Mersey and is now beautifully landscaped.

Turn left under the stone bridge arch and walk through The Dell to the end where steps will head back to the station which you will see in front of you to complete the walk.

Dibbinsdale

THIS delightful walk takes you around Dibbinsdale and Brotherton Park, a haven for birds and other wildlife amongst the maze of footpaths. You also visit St. Patrick's Well and the recently opened visitor centre.

Start: *Dibbinsdale Local Nature Reserve off Spital Road, Bromborough. Grid ref: 346 827.*

Distance: *2.5 km/1¼ miles.*

Parking: *Car park near the Ranger's Office and Visitor Centre.*

Refreshments: *Ideal place for a picnic.*

Points of Interest: *Dibbinsdale Local Nature Reserve; St. Patrick's Well.*

The walk

Walk back to the car park entrance (house opposite) turn right and walk along the access road. Bear right at a fork by a terrace of houses to arrive at a small turning area beside the Rangers Office and Visitor Centre with its walled garden. (You are advised to telephone the Ranger on 0151 334 9851 to check opening times if you are going to visit it.)

From the Visitor Centre, retrace your steps for a few yards along the access road and turn left by a small information board. The path is forked here—take the left fork ignoring paths on either side. After a wooden bench continue a little further to a crossing of paths. Go ahead out of the woods briefly on a descending path and soon you will be walking above the river down to your right. There is a viewpoint at post 2 giving views into the valley. Continue ahead descending until you reach a

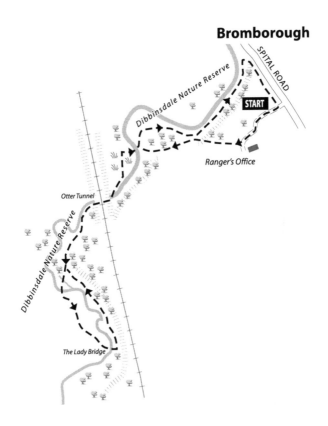

wooden footbridge on the left. Cross the bridge and take the first path on the left at post 3.

Note the swampy ground either side of the path and the tall 'Norfolk Reeds', traditionally grown and cut in the Norfolk Fens for thatching roofs. It is a very productive British plant, growing a new crop of stems each year from the roots. This area provides an excellent habitat for birds such as reed and sedge warblers, moorhens, reed buntings, teal, mallards and the occasional over-wintering water rail.

Cross the river by a footbridge and follow the path through a tunnel beneath the railway, known as the 'Otter Tunnel'. As you emerge from the tunnel bear left and follow the path close to

Dibbinsdale

river down to the right. At a fork in the path bear right crossing two bridges to post 6.

Turn left here and walk along the path with a meadow on your right, named as Boden's Hey on the Tithe map of 1840.

The grass is cut and baled in summer as part of a meadow restoration scheme. Without this cutting, the meadow would become scrub with less wildlife value.

In front of you and to your left is Marford's Wood, an ancient woodland owned by the Lancelyn-Green family but managed by Wirral Borough Council on a 'peppercorn' rent of one acorn per year. It forms part of Dibbinsdale's Site of Special Scientific Interest (SSSI). This wood was once part of the medieval Forest of Wirral, an area looked after by the Forester of Wirral for hunting purposes. His emblem was the Wirral Horn

At a path junction bear left to cross a footbridge and 'The Lady Bridge', to arrive at steep steps in front of you. Ignore these and turn left here. Follow this path, keeping the river on your left and bearing right where you crossed the river earlier (by the two bridges to reach post 6). Continue along this path to the tunnel. Go back through the tunnel under the railway and at the other end, cross the river by the footbridge and continue along the path to a T junction (post 3).

Turn right at the T junction, cross the wooden footbridge and bear left almost immediately where the path forks. Continue along this path passing beneath a sandstone outcrop on your right with the river close by on your left.

Contiue on the footpath above the river. A few yards after a sleeper bridge over a small stream and well before you reach the main road, turn sharp right to arrive at St Patrick's Well.

The well is supposed to be associated with the arrival of St Patrick from Ireland in 432 A.D when he is said to have blessed the well, causing it to have special healing powers for the eyes. However, this feature has only appeared on the first O.S. map (1860s) and probably only dates from this time.

Continue on over a little stone footbridge and turn left up a small valley to return to the car cark to complete the walk.

WALK 23

Raby

A short walk along quiet lanes and field paths centred on Wirral's smallest village—a handful of cottages and old farm buildings plus one of the prettiest pubs—the 17th century 'Wheatsheaf Inn'—with its thatched roof and cosy rooms.

Start: *The 'Wheatsheaf Inn', Raby. Grid ref: 311 798.*

Distance: *3.5km/2½ miles.*

Parking: *'The Green', Raby by the 'Wheatsheaf Inn'.*

Refreshments: *The 'Wheatsheaf Inn' open every day from 11.30am to 11pm for drinks and from 10.30am on Sundays. Food served from 12noon to 2pm and from 6pm except Sunday evening and Mondays. Excellent for Sunday lunches.*

Points of Interest: *'Wheatsheaf Inn', Raby.*

In 1891, the Wheatsheaf Inn had one bed for travellers and a catering facility for 10 people according to the Register of Licensed Houses. Compare that with the number it can cater for nowadays.

The walk

From the 'Wheatsheaf Inn' turn left and walk to the end of 'The Green'. Turn left again and walk along the lane, passing a road on your left after 600 yards. Continue ahead until you see a main road (B5151) ahead. Turn right here onto a footpath enclosed between hedges.

Follow this footpath eventually passing a house on your left, then 'Roselea Farm'. Here, immediately before the road, turn right through a metal kissing gate and walk along the edge of a field. Near the top corner of the field look for a stile on your right

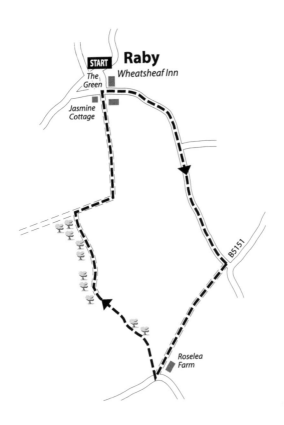

and cross over it into a narrow strip of woodland. Turn left and follow the path through the trees until you come to a T-junction with another path at the end of the wood (about ½ mile).

Notice the gateposts either side of the path—obviously the entrance to a large property at some time in the past.

Turn right and follow the path to reach a stile onto a farm track. Cross the stile, turn left and follow this farm track back to Raby passing 'Jasmine Cottage' just before the lane. Go ahead now back to the 'Wheatsheaf Inn' to complete the walk.

Willaston

A walk around the village of Willaston and the surrounding fields centered on the old Hadlow Road station on the Wirral Way. This has been restored to its days as a working station before the 1950s.

Start: *Hadlow Road station on the Wirral Way. Grid ref: 331 774.*

Distance: *4km/2½ miles.*

Parking: *At Hadlow Road station where there is a free car park for the Wirral Way.*

Refreshments: *'Pollards Inn' for bar meals every day, children's menu and Sunday lunches. Phone 0151 327 4615 for opening times. Play area.*

Points of Interest: *Hadlow Road station, Willaston Old Hall, The Old Mill.*

The walk

Turn right out of the car park and walk along the road to the centre of the village.

At the T junction turn left and walk along to the church. Immediately before the church turn right onto a path by the cemetery. At the end of the path turn left, then right into 'Mill Green'. Immediately before the first house on the left turn left onto a path which passes behind the house to playing fields. Go ahead up the righthand side of the following fields to 'Mill Lane'.

Turn right along the lane passing the 'Old Mill'. Follow the road round the bend and look for a signposted public footpath which follows a track on left immediately before the first house. Turn right with the track and at a large gate follow the enclosed footpath to the right. At an access road continue ahead, a little to the left on a footpath between gardens to emerge on the road by a petrol station.

Turn left, cross the road and go along 'Change Lane' on the right. When the lane bends to the left, cross the stile on your right and go ahead across the following fields. After the third field pass between bungalows to emerge in a small cul de sac. Turn left out of the cul de sac to the end of 'Pemberton Close' and turn right. At the T junction ('Moss Close') turn left and walk along 'Old Vicarage Lane". At the end of the road a footpath leads ahead to 'Hadlow Road'.

Just before you reach 'Hadlow Road', turn left along a rough access road ('Smithy Lane'). Continue along 'Smithy Lane' until

it passes beween horse paddocks. Take the signed footpath on the right here ('Adfalent Lane') which leads down to the Wirral Way. Turn right along the Wirral Way and return to the car park by Hadlow Road Station.

The station, which closed in 1952, has been restored and refurbished. There are toilets inside the station building.

Willaston is an attractive country village and well worth a look around if you can spare the time. It is believed to be one of the earliest settlements of the invading Anglo-Saxons in Wirral.

Old Willaston Mill is just a tower now — the last of several mills in the area some dating back to the 14th century. Legend has it that one old Willaston miller was so efficient that he had the corn cut and threshed in the early hours of the morning, immediately grinding it and making it into bread, then delivered it to London the same night!!

Willaston Mill

Parkgate

A walk along the edge of the Dee marshes to Gayton with a return to Parkgate along the Wirral Way. It will be enjoyed by birdwatchers, especially when the tides are at their highest, and for children, with the promise of icecream at the end to spur them on!

Start: *In the public car park beyond the 'Boathouse Inn' at the northern end of 'The Parade', Parkgate. Grid ref: 274 790.*

Distance: *5.5km/3½ miles.*

Parking: *In the public car park beyond the 'Boathouse Inn'*

Refreshments: *'Boathouse Inn' or numerous restaurants, pubs or cafés along 'The Parade'.*

Points of Interest: *Bird watching from the car park especially at high tide; The Ropewalk; Mostyn House School.*

The walk

Walk through the car park (away from Parkgate) and along the footpath which follows the old sea wall.

At the lane end by 'Gayton Cottage' turn right down the steps and walk up the road to the bridge. Cross the bridge and turn right here down the path to join the Wirral Way. Turn left away from the bridge and follow the Wirral Way back towards Parkgate.

In approximately 1 mile you can shorten the walk by going right at the first bridge (Blackwood Hall Bridge). This will take you back to the car park, otherwise continue passing under a second bridge to the third bridge, this takes you over rather than under the road. Cross the bridge and go down steps on your right. Turn left at the bottom and walk past the Primary

School. Continue down the road to a footpath on the left known as 'Ropewalk'.

This straight path was once used by rope makers to stretch out their ropes.

Turn left and follow 'Ropewalk' past a children's playground on the left to a crossing footpath. Turn right here, cross the road and walk down the path opposite alongside Mostyn House School playing field to join 'Little Lane' which emerges on the old sea front ('The Parade').

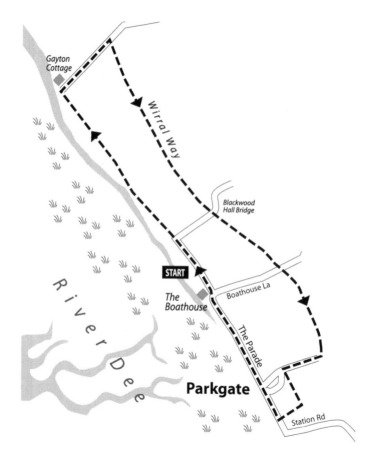

'The Parade', the old sea front at Parkgate

Turn right and walk back along 'The Parade' but not before you've treated yourself to a Nicholls' home-made ice-cream or bought some shrimps to take home with you. Don't be surprised if you have to queue for the ice cream as customers come from far and wide, even in winter.

Continue on along 'The Parade' to the end past the 'Boathouse Inn' to the car park to complete the walk.

Neston

AN interesting walk starting in Neston and leading down beside
the old marshes to the delightful Harp Inn.

Start: *Car park near the station. Grid ref: 292 776.*

Distance: *5km/3 miles.*

Parking: *Public car park in 'Raby Road' by the station. There is also a
large car park near the junction of 'Raby Road' and 'Ladies Walk'.*

Refreshments: *'Brewer's Arms' or 'Harp Inn' (down on the
marshes).*

Points of Interest: *Neston Cross; Neston parish churchyard; the Old
Quay; the Harp Inn.*

The walk

Turn left out of the car park by the station and bear right along
'Raby Road' to the traffic lights. Turn right here, then bear left
immediately past the 'Brewer's Arms' on your left. Continue a
little further passing 'Churchill Way' and turn left down 'Mill
Street'. Walk down the lane to the road at the bottom. Cross the
main road and turn right passing the library and the garden.
Turn left onto the footpath immediately after the garden. At
the end of the path cross a road and continue on down the path
opposite to the Wirral Way. Cross the Wirral Way and continue
to a T junction with a lane.

Turn right here and walk along the tarmac road, passing the
'Old Laundry' on your left. At the next road junction turn left
and walk down the road, then a path in front of you to reach the
marshes. Follow a narrow path left here along the edge of the
marshes.

Cross a stile into a more open area then cross a stream by a narrow wooden footbridge.

Note the remains of the Old Quay on your right (part of a stone wall) where ships set sail for Ireland in the days when the water came right up to the edge of the fields here and before the river became silted up. Coal was the main cargo in those days from the nearby Neston Colliery. This is a good spot for birdwatching.

Cross a stone stile then continue ahead until you come to houses/bungalows and immediately after these is the 'Harp Inn' which serves good food, real ale or even just a cup of tea or coffee.

Note the old pictures on the walls plus miners' lamps, pick axe etc. to commemorate the local coal mining.

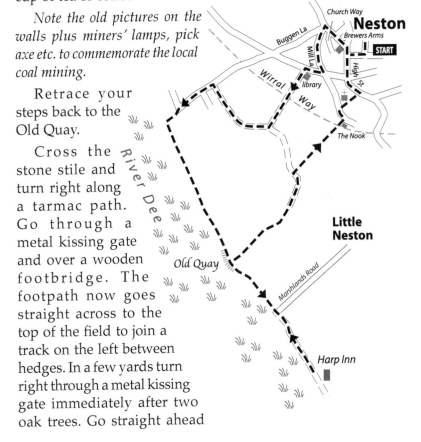

Retrace your steps back to the Old Quay.

Cross the stone stile and turn right along a tarmac path. Go through a metal kissing gate and over a wooden footbridge. The footpath now goes straight across to the top of the field to join a track on the left between hedges. In a few yards turn right through a metal kissing gate immediately after two oak trees. Go straight ahead along the main path through the following fields to cross over the Wirral Way and come up a path by 'The Nook'. Turn left along the tarmac lane and at the church turn right to walk through the churchyard.

Have a look around to find coal miner's graves and others of interest. Can you find the one of a husband who died aged 12! Obviously a mistake.

Walk past the church and leave by the front gates. Turn left. You are now in the centre of Neston where you will see the Cross ahead of you.

Before 1820, Neston was the only town in Wirral and it is mentioned in the Domesday book.

Continue ahead past the cross and turn right into 'Raby Road' by the traffic lights to return to the car park.

The Harp Inn, Little Neston

Burton

A short, easy walk around picturesque Burton and the small woodland which backs the village.

Start: *At the Gladstone Village Hall, Burton. Grid ref: 318 744.*

Distance: *3km/2 miles.*

Parking: *In the main street or in the grounds of Burton Manor if going there for lunch.*

Refreshments: *Tea and coffee available at Burton Manor. Sunday lunch can be enjoyed at Burton Manor but must be booked in advance (tel: 0151 336 5172).*

Points of Interest: *Quaker Graves; Hampston's Well; parish church.*

The walk

From 'Gladstone Village Hall' turn right along the road, away from the centre of the village, then take the first left into 'Vicarage Lane', a bridleway and public footpath. Turn left again along another footpath by 'Haddon Lodge' and 'Wood Close'. Just before reaching the church turn right and follow a woodland path. *The Quaker Graves on your right date from 1663.*

Continue on through the woods, passing a sign for 'Burton Wood' on the right. The path veers uphill now to the right then opens out. Bear left here, then continue straight ahead close by a fence on the left. Continue until you reach a low wall with a signed path to the left. Ignore this path but cross the wall then go straight ahead along 'Mill Lane' to the road.

Turn left and proceed along the pavement back towards Burton. When the pavement ends, opposite 'Bank House' continue ahead on the footpath and down steps into 'Station Road'. Turn right and enjoy an excellent view of the 'new' Dee Bridge.

A short distance along 'Station Road' will bring you to Hampston's Well.

The remains of the well were restored in 1975 and a garden was made by Ellesmere Port Borough Council as a tribute to the memory of Councillor Horace Edgar Green who died in 1973 aged 86 years.

It is believed the well possibly served Iron Age settlements at Burton Point and an Anglo-Saxon settlement at Burton about 900A.D. The earliest known written records date from 1602-3 in the manor court book in which it is referred to as Patrick's Well. There are frequent references regarding the upkeep of the well. The constables of Burton were charged with cleaning the well every year and all able bodied men of Burton were required to help or pay a fine of 6d. The washing of clothes at the well was prohibited, also the turning of the well water from its course. It became known as Hampston's Well by the 19th century after a family who had lived at Burton since the 16th century.

Cottages in Burton

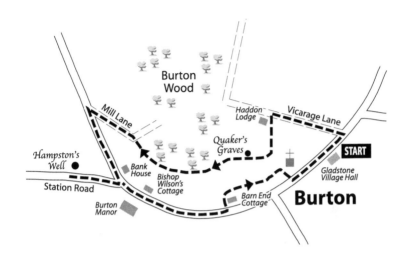

Retrace your steps along 'Station Road' and continue into the village.

It's hard to imagine but this sleepy little village actually acquired a market charter in 1298. Now even its last remaining shop, that of butcher has closed down although a Post Office is still here three mornings a week.

Pass 'Burton Manor' and 'Bishop Wilson's Cottage' with its thatched roof.

Thomas Wilson was born in Burton in 1663. He was educated at the King's School in Chester and Trinity College, Dublin. In 1697 he became Bishop of Sodor and Man, a post he retained for 58 years. He was very generous and self-sacrificing and called himself the poorest bishop in Europe! The village school is named after him.

Turn left up the signed footpath by 'Barn End'. Behind the cottages turn right along an access road to the church.

There are some interesting gravestones in the churchyard. Go down the main path and down the steps to the road. Turn left and walk back to 'Gladstone Village Hall' to complete the walk.

Shotwick

Beginning at the sleepy backwater of Shotwick with its old cottages and even older church, this short easy walk crosses the fields to the village of Puddington with a return to Shotwick.

Start: *Shotwick church. Grid ref: 337 718.*

Distance: *5km/3 miles.*

Parking: *By the church in the centre of Shotwick.*

Refreshments: *No cafés or pubs so take a picnic.*

Points of Interest: *Church; Cross in the churchyard by the gate; Victorian (VR) Post Box; Shotwick Hall.*

It is worth looking in the church before you start or at the end of the walk as it has some interesting features including box pews dating from 1710. Outside in the porch can be found grooves which are said to have been made by archers sharpening their arrows for archery practice after Mass on Sundays. Other accounts say that it was Cheshire archers en-route to battle in Ireland who made the grooves.

The walk

Walk back along the road away from the church, noting some of the lovely old houses and cottages. Pass the Victorian letter box and turn left into 'Hall Lane'. Continue along the lane ignoring the left turn.

Pass Shotwick Hall and farm, a beautiful old house dating from 1662 and continue ahead to a gate where the path turns left in front of the gate then narrows between two hedges. Ignore a left turn and continue along this narrow path. Go through a gate at the end of the path and straight on across the field and across the next

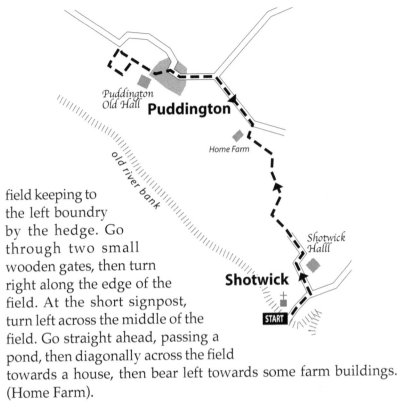

field keeping to
the left boundry
by the hedge. Go
through two small
wooden gates, then turn
right along the edge of the
field. At the short signpost,
turn left across the middle of the
field. Go straight ahead, passing a
pond, then diagonally across the field
towards a house, then bear left towards some farm buildings.
(Home Farm).

Turn right along a concrete track by the farm buildings and
at the road bear left. Follow the road between houses to the
end near the entrance to a drive leading to 'Puddington Hall'.
Turn left along the road ('Puddington Lane') and follow this to
Puddington.

*The village green is a good place for your picnic, especially under
the spreading chestnut trees.*

Turn left from the green by the 'Old Forge 1834', then left
again into 'Old Hall Lane' and walk to the end. Turn left along
a green footpath to the end, then left again to bring you back to
'Puddington Lane'.

Turn right and retrace your steps back to Shotwick.

Shotwick Church

The path beside the church leads to the old ford across the River Dee into Wales which was well established by the Middle Ages as a route for salt (from the mid-Cheshire salt workings) into North Wales. In 1245, Henry III passed through Shotwick with his army as did Edward I in 1278 and 1284.

By the end of the 15th century, the River Dee was too silted up for ships to go to Chester so Shotwick (probably from the nearby castle) became the major port of Chester. Until relatively recently (1970s) there were rings in the churchyard wall said to have been used for mooring ships and boats but these have now disappeared.

WALK *29*

Capenhurst

A very easy short circular walk through the village and across farmland.

Start: *Capenhurst church. Grid ref: 368 737.*

Distance: *3.75km/2¼ miles.*

Parking: *Limited parking by the church or along the road in the village.*

Refreshments: *None in the village but 'The Old Wirral Hundred' pub on the main A41 road has a beer garden and a childrens' play area.*

Points of Interest: *Village pinfold.*

The walk

From the church walk left along the road, passing the school on the right and the old pinfold restored by the Parish Council.

Continue along the road until you reach the entrance to 'Atkinson Tractors Ltd' on the right.

Turn left over a stile (to the left of 'Keeper's Cottage') immediately after the entrance onto a field path. Follow the footpath ahead, crossing several fields and stiles to reach a narrow woodland. Go ahead through the wood to join a farm track and follow this until it swings rightwards. Cross a stile ahead and follow the right of way beside a house to reach the road.

Turn right along the road, passing a large metal storage barn and 'Ashcroft Farmhouse' where the new road bears left. Walk ahead along the old lane (Powley Lane) passing 'Rendova Farm', until you reach the main A540 road. Turn right along the footpath to Gibbet Mill on the right.

Sometime in the 18th century, three Irish harvesters quarrelled over their earnings and the one with the largest share was murdered by the other two. These two, then stopped at The Greyhound Inn at Shotwick and attempted to rob the landlady. Caught in the act, they were arrested and imprisoned at Chester where they confessed to the murder of their companion. They were tried and executed and, in accordance with the custom of the time, their bodies were hung in chains or 'gibbeted' near the scene of their crime – in this case, from an ash tree that grew close to the mill – as a warning to others. Since then, Saughall Mill has been known locally as–' The Gibbet Mill'.

Climb over a stile on your right immediately after the drive to the mill. Walk ahead through the field passing the mill and cross a small stile in a fence. Turn right now to cross a second stile, then turn left along the field edge. Cross a stile and footbridge in the bottom corner of the field and bear half-left passing a concrete pillar. Immediately before a large field gate ahead, bear left along an overgrown track with a bank to the left and hedge and field to the right. Follow this track to the road. Turn right along the road and walk back through the village to complete the walk

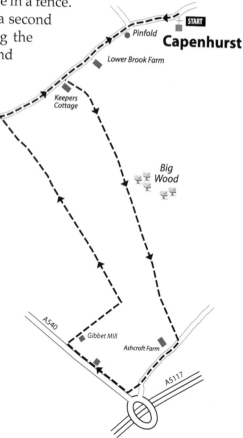

90

Hooton & Rivacre Valley

A woodland walk to Rivacre Valley Country Park and back using good woodland paths in the country park and rights of way across the golf course.

Start: *St. Paul's Church car park. Hooton. Grid ref: 363 783.*

Distance: *4km/2½ miles.*

Parking: *Turn off the A41 opposite Burleydam Nursery to St. Paul's Church in Hooton. Drive past the church to the end of the short access road and park in the little car park near the golf club.*

Refreshments: *Burleydam Nursery or picnic in the country park.*

Points of Interest: *Rivacre Valley Country Park; Borewell Station No. 2.*

The walk

From the car park go through the kissing gate into 'Church Wood' and follow a path to pass between two ponds. Turn right at a T junction immediately after the ponds to the golf course.

Turn left and follow white marker posts along edge of the golf course. At a footbridge on the left, cross over and bear right to walk between two strips of woodland. At the end of the trees bear right across the golf course to a gravel footpath and follow this to pass through a mesh fence by benches. Turn left by the benches into the woods.

Follow a woodland path to the right (there is more than one but they all go in the same direction) along the edge of the woods until it swings right into an open area with houses ahead and a fingerpost. Turn left and follow the path down to cross over 'Crossway Bridge'. Turn left up the rising path which soon runs parallel to a road with houses on the right. Continue to the road.

Turn right for a few yards then cross the road and enter Rivacre Valley Country Park. Walk across the car park towards the Ranger's office. (Call in for information about the Country Park or telephone: 0151 357 1991.) Go up steps to the right of the office and follow the path leftwards. Turn left through a fence by more houses, then turn immediately left to go down to an access road. Cross the road keeping left at a fork and continue over a bridge. Turn left along a path which will bring you to a road by Borewell Station No.2 (Bridgewater Paper Co.).

The unusual building here is a pumping station (one of six old wells) which reach deep into the ground. Water is still extracted from them for use by the paper mill.

Cross the lane and take the footpath opposite. This woodland path will bring you back to 'Crossway Bridge'. Turn right and retrace your outward route through the wood, over the golf course and back through Church Wood between the ponds to the car park to complete the walk.

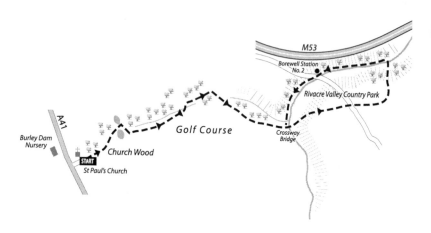

Borewell Station No.2

Mara Books

Mara Books publish a range of walking books for Cheshire and North Wales and have the following list to date. A complete list of current titles is available on our web site:

www.marabooks.co.uk *or*
www.northerneyebooks.com

North Wales

Coastal Walks around Anglesey

ISBN 978-1-902512-20-4. A collection of 22 circular walks exploring the coast of Anglesey, designated an Area of Outstanding Natural Beauty.

Official Guide to The Isle of Anglesey Coastal Path

ISBN 978-1-902512-13-6. An official guide to the new coastal path. Bi-lingual and full colour throughout.

Walking on the Lleyn Peninsula

ISBN 978-1-902512-15-0. New edition. A collection of circular walks exploring the wild and beautiful coastline and hills of the Lleyn Peninsula.

Circular Walks in the Conwy Valley

ISBN 978-1-902512-11-2. New edition. A collection of circular walks which explore the varied scenery of this beautiful valley from the Great Orme to Betws-y-Coed.

Walking in Snowdonia *Volume 1*

ISBN 978-1-902512-06-8. A series of circular walks exploring the beautiful and dramatic valleys in the northern half of the Snowdonia National Park.

A pocket guide to Snowdon

ISBN 978-1-902512-16-7. A guide to all the recognised routes of ascent, from the six 'Classic Paths' to the many lesser known and less frequented routes. Includes a full colour relief map.

A pocket guide to Snowdonia's best Mountain Walks

ISBN 978-1-902512-19-8. A guide to the best walks and scrambles to be enjoyed in the mountains of the Snowdownia National Park.

Walking in the Clwydian Range

ISBN 978-1-902512-14-3. A collection of 18 circular walks exploring the Clwydian Range Area of Outstanding Natural Beauty (AONB).

Cheshire

Circular Walks along the Sandstone Trail

ISBN 978-1-902512-21-1. New edition. The Sandstone Trail is Cheshire's best known and most popular walking route. This book gives a complete route description along with 12 circular walks covering the entire trail.

A Walker's Guide to the Wirral Shore Way

ISBN 1 902512 05 7. This book describes a linear walk of 23 miles following the old coastline between Chester and Hoylake.

Circular Walks in Wirral

ISBN 978-1-902512-22-8. A collection of circular walks in the coast and countryside of Wirral.

About the author

Joanna McIlhatton was introduced to the delights of walking by her parents and has loved it ever since. When her husband-to-be took her rock climbing, she found it terrifying and decided to stick to mountain walking. Later, when her husband was made redundant, they opened a shop together in Wirral, selling walking boots and waterproof clothing and were able to offer advice based on personal experience which was well received.

When Joanna lost her husband, she bought an old farmhouse near Cerrigydrudion on the edge of Snowdonia in North Wales and converted the barns into luxurious bunkhouse accommodation. She was able to take parties of people out walking then come back and cook dinner for her guests, a lifestyle she loved.

Nowadays, Joanna is back living in Wirral and being slightly disabled, she prefers the shorter walks of her local area, hence the reason for writing this book.

She is a founder member of the Riverside Writer's Group in West Kirby. Her other writing includes a walking guide to the villages of the Hiraethog area of Denbighshire, plus two cookery books and she is in the process of completing a book entitled: *Wonderful Wirral, First and Foremost*, which lists the achievements made over the years to which Wirral can lay claim, either nationally or internationally, and over one hundred items have been included. She also intends to complete a novel by next year.